LESS STRESS, M

8. Okt. 2008

With compliments of an extra Figurant.

LESS STRESS, MORE SUCCESS!

A rare collection of stress-busters and tips to live, love and enjoy life

Christian Worth

ISBN : 1-4196-5310-5

To order additional copies, please contact us.
BookSurge, LLC
www.booksurge.com
1-866-308-6235
orders@booksurge.com

LESS STRESS, MORE SUCCESS!

THIS IS FOR YOU!

Wisdom that is not shared is wasted.

So I wrote this book. Some people asked me to. Friends, colleagues, acquaintances, people attending my seminars, and finally a publisher.

The wisdom I refer to is acquired. I was not born a wise man but hundreds, thousands of people collaborated to offer it to me. This is an attempt to share it.

I was lucky enough through adolescence and through my adult life to experience many challenging situations and to be able to note, as I went, the lessons of this wonderful rollercoaster.

I grew up with a squint and never got used to people turning around to find out who I was looking at!

Fortunately it stopped when I was 16 thanks to the able hands of an eye surgeon in Paris. When the stressful fear of not making contact with other people went away, I discovered how much it had handicapped my early years.

At 19, I acted in a student production that represented France in the International University Theatre Festival in Nancy, France. The magic of theatre always fascinated me and I thought that it would be lots of fun. Very probably, I also wanted to see the audience looking at me. The success of that production confirmed that I had been right in challenging my fears.

During my National Military Service I was draughted as a private soldier instead of trainee officer, due to peculiar calendar reasons and I ended-up teaching reading and writing to some fellow soldiers. I enjoyed that very much!

That 1964 winter I became a military ski instructor and together with that position came freedom and power but also responsibility. I had to teach my fellow soldiers something that I had acquired instinctively. Stressful, yes but also a great opportunity!

In my life in Advertising, I was asked to work on many product categories, from mattresses to beer, feminine hygiene, veterinary products, airlines, electronic toy organs, deodorant soaps, floor cleaners, all temperature laundry detergents, telecommunications, chemical products, chocolate bars, chewing gum and cheese. It required a curious mind and taking all the challenges of learning about these new product categories in my stride.

To simplify things, Young & Rubicam, my employer expatriated me from France to Mexico, to Italy, to Quebec, to Japan, to Germany, Japan again and finally to Hong Kong which is the temple of stress. Obviously, my family followed these moves and for 30 years was regularly uprooted and plunged in new unfamiliar places, meeting new people and negotiating our sanity to blend in the local, perfectly normal but often challenging ways of life.

So Stress there was, and fortunately Success too.

Fortunately also, from my early childhood and the eye problem, I had developed a keen interest for what makes people act, for what causes things to happen and what makes people react the way they do. All during these years of exposure to stressful situations, I observed and made mental notes.

Today, as a Life and Business Coach, I get to help my clients find their way through the daily obstacle course to a life with less Stress and more Success. What a joy!

So this book is a Nippo-Canado-Mexico-Italo-Franco-Sino-Anglo cocktail of stress busters and survival tips. If you should only find one tip that you will use, the effort of writing this book would be justified.

This book and the tips in it are for you to enjoy.

October 2006.
Haitzpean
– St Pée sur Nivelle, France.

WHY LESS STRESS?

Some stress is good for us.

It comes from stimulation. It is our response to it.

The key is to have stimulation that makes us respond positively.

Most people do not object to stimulation but everyone objects to suffering from the stress.

It is a challenge to develop ways to enjoy and welcome the stimulation but without the pain of the stress, without the tensions in the body, the anxieties in the mind.

You have the power.

Together we shall confirm that you have a lot of power to decide what you want to experience and what you don't want to be subjected to. You just have to be aware of it, decide to use it and indeed use that power

> *"If you are pained by external things, it is not they that disturb you, but your own judgment of them and it is in your power to wipe out that judgment now".*
>
> - *Marcus Aurelius.*-

Your Tools

You have many ways to minimize the negative impact of stressful moments on your life.

We shall talk about what you can do with **Your Powerful Mind**. That is where it all starts. The aspirations, the ideas, the expectations, the decisions, the filters applied to the perceptions, all contribute to your satisfaction or your frustration. And where there are frustrated expectations, there is stress.

We shall work on where stress ends-up: **Your Body.**

The tensions, the aches and pains, the unconscious accumulation of upsetting events take their toll and that impacts on how your mind is able to work to manage all the rest:

"Mens sana in corpore sano"

We shall consider the areas where you can take action and use your power to fight back and keep your body relaxed and fit. You deserve it.

Your Environment has an enormous impact on how you feel and how you are able to act. You will be invited to have another look at whether it works for or against you.

The office environment may be easier to influence than you think.

Your home is yours to arrange how you feel and how it best supports your goal.

Your Relationships can make you or destroy you. Whether at work or in your private life, what you do to other people impacts on what they do to you. The way you relate to people and treat them conditions the way they treat you. Without exception.

Some of the ways you impact on people around you are unintentional, and some are intentional. The more you can control this impact on others, the better.

Let us work on it together.

It is that easy to live with Less Stress.

WHAT SUCCESS?

You may have bought this book because you could do with additional success?

This book will help anyone to be more successful. However you will have to define what success is for you. I cannot do that for you, as I do not know you personally. In my Coaching work with clients we work on their specific goals.

Here is a quote attributed to Michael Jordan:

"Vision without action is a daydream.
Action without vision is a nightmare.
I've missed 9000 shots in my career. I've lost more than 300 games.
Twenty-six times I've been trusted to take the game winning shot
and missed. I've failed over and over and over again in my life.
And that is why I succeed."

Michael Jordan, The Chicago Bulls

So this book has very little specifically written on how to succeed. It will have absolutely nothing original from me on what success is. Who am I to know whether, for you, success is managing to change a damaged tap in your bathroom, getting a smile on the face of someone in despair or inventing a new computer software?

Allow me to share with you a few more quotes about success in order to cast a little more light on the topic.

Success is a state of mind'

"SUCCESS COMES IN CANS......NOT CAN'TS!"

"The people who get on in this world are the people who get up and look for the circumstances they want, and, if they can't find them, make them."
- George Bernard Shaw

"Success is largely a matter of hanging on
after others have let go"

"The two secrets of success are:
Never tell anyone everything you know.
First, have fun.
Second, love your work.
Third, go in the opposite direction to everyone else."

- Anita Roddick

To laugh often and much; to win the respect of intelligent people and the affection of children; to earn the appreciation of honest critics and endure the betrayal of false friends; to appreciate beauty; to find the best in others; to leave the world a little bit better, whether by a healthy child, a garden patch or a redeemed social condition; to know even one life has breathed easier because you have lived.
This is to have succeeded.
-Ralph Waldo Emerson

PART ONE

YOUR POWERFUL MIND.

Yours!... and Beautiful!

Your mind is the source of all your actions.
Your mind is the receptacle of all your sensations.
Your mind will interpret all your perceptions and draw the conclusions that will get you going in one direction or the other.

And you can influence this process to help your mind to drive you in the right direction.

"Whether you think you can, or you think you can't – you are right."
- Henry Ford (1863 - 1947)

The things that are important to you shape your decisions.

Your values shape your actions.

The people who paint graffiti have different values to those who own the wall they paint on. Very simple conclusion!

What is less simple to grasp and accept is that sometimes we act in a way which conflicts with our own values. We do things that are not in line with what we think is right, with our values, and although we may not be conscious of that conflict, it is there and it nags and weakens us. It is a source of stress.

So in fighting the negative side effects of stress we shall try and identify where we may have such invisible sources of stress.

Your needs are powerful factors in determining what you do and don't do, what you are prepared to accept graciously and what irks you. Knowing your needs better and working at having them met will make a world of difference on how you react to what is happening around you.

Your mind can work to deliver such apparently mind boggling ideas as:

- "Bliss on purpose"
- "The Present is Perfect!"

It all starts with a clear awareness of what is happening and how that is in line with what you want.

Let's start.

BUST YOUR TOLERATIONS

How serene are you?

Cultivating serenity starts with dealing with tolerations.

Imagine that your serenity would be represented by a big bowl where some liquid rests peacefully. Just like a lake, or a pond, its beauty is in the stillness, in the constant level.

There would be something wrong in a lake or a pond partially full.

Now imagine that there be a pinhole in the bowl, through which the liquid seeps. It would not stay serenely full. In order to keep it full, you would have to replenish the content from time to time. Serenity would be incomplete otherwise.

Should there be many pinholes and cracks in the bowl, you would have to refill vigorously and frequently and there would be no serenity at all. Refilling the bowl could become a full time activity.

What is the solution?

Prevent the draining of the bowl! Plug the holes, fix the cracks! This is the condition for serenity.

The strength of this bowl image is in the identifying that the draining factors are tiny, easy to ignore, but their accumulation has a disastrous effect on the content.

The pinholes in the bowl are our "tolerations" in our daily life. They are these little things that we do not like, which irritate us to a small extent and that we have become so used to that we ignore them. Still they are there, we notice them, albeit unconsciously and they drain our energy:

- The leaking tap,
- The squeaky door,
- The TV on during meals,
- The messy garden,
- The obnoxious behaviour,
- The clutter on the desk,
- The smoker at the next table,
- The clothes on the floor,
- The inadequate lighting,
- The uncomfortable mattress,
- The noisy environment,
- The boring job,
- The old wallpaper,
- The chipped plate or cup,
- Etc,

We tolerate and, without even being aware of it, we compensate for the corresponding drain in order not to feel too bad. We refill the bowl at the top with something that gives us a little pleasure;

- A cigarette,
- A cup of coffee,
- A snack,
- A drink,
- An ice-cream,
- A little retail therapy,
- A selfish attitude,
- A sharp wisecracking word,
- An affair,

- A new something,
- A new someone ....

These little pleasures are not very good for our health, our relationships or our finances and it would be far better to go to the source, the tolerations and deal with them.

STOP TOLERATING!

In the following table identify all the things that you are currently tolerating. You have space for 15 but you can use an extra sheet of paper.

Toleration	Action	Date
-		
-		
-		
-		
-		
-		
-		
-		
-		
-		
-		
-		
-		
-		

Then write the action that you can take to zap that toleration. Finally select three easy ones and write a date at which you will deal with each of them.

Make it a point to zap one or more a day until they are ALL gone!

Less Tolerations = Less Stress = More Serenity

What if I cannot eliminate a toleration ?

If you feel that you cannot eliminate it, think twice and

talk to somebody about it. Maybe there is a way that is difficult for you to perceive from where you are.

In many circumstances, it is a wise move to call upon someone to help you to clarify your situation and help you identify what you can do about that situation. That help can relate to the way you perceive the toleration, or it can be about how you can gently get rid of that toleration.

Your personal coach is the ideal partner to discuss these themes, identify tolerations and their solutions. Your coach will also keep you company in your efforts to eradicate the toleration.

If busting that toleration is truly and absolutely out of reach for you, even by indirect means, you may want to eliminate it by accepting it. It will take a special effort but it will be worth it.

ACCEPTING WHAT IS.

If it rains or the weather is grey, you cannot do anything about it.

There is a reason why you are in this climate.

There is a reason why it is raining.

Your best bet is to decide what you can do about the situation. Rain is a fact.

You may rationalise that we need water, or that it is good for the garden, etc.

Or you can opt for a good activity indoors,

Or you can go on a vacation to a sunny place.

Stopping the rain is beyond your control.

Accept what is and focus on something within your control.

BLISS ON PURPOSE

"Ignorance is Bliss! "... Is it really?

That sentence does not suggest an active search for the state of bliss though!

Is there a way to seek bliss, so as to magnify the potential for bliss in our life? Definitely!

Bliss is often defined as "perfect happiness".

Happiness is having the world as you like it and feeling 'in the flow'.

Does this mean that the world has to be still and that we have to be suspended in a big vacuum? Certainly not! It is more a matter of being in harmony with what is happening.

So "Bliss on Purpose" is a personal strategy. It is the expression of a strong will.

A friend of mine reflected recently on the fact that I am rarely ill. I honestly answered that it may come from the fact that I do not want to be ill. To what extent is this a silly, arrogant statement? Would you have answered the same way I did?

I sense that arrogance enters for very little in the statement. Optimism and Positive Mental Attitude play a bigger role.

I believe in it. I have my share of colds and aches, but overall less than the average. I enjoy what I am, and with the skilful help of my delightful wife, I do not fall ill.

REJOICE

Rejoice" is not just a word for Christmas Cards.

It is an attitude through which you notice the good things in life and celebrate them.

It is a determination to go for the good side of anything and savour it.

In 1999 we took time out for a skiing holiday. I love skiing and looked forward to being in the snow again, renting modern equipment and discovering all the new techniques.

On the first day we rented the equipment and took the lifts to the top of Les Arcs to meet our friends at the "restaurant d'altitude". Gorgeous sunny views and superb snow. Pure delight!

We planted the skis in the snow bank along the "terrasse" outside and went inside for a friendly meal. When I came out, my skis were gone, taken by someone else. I looked everywhere.

- *"Someone had mistaken their skis for yours"*, said the restaurant owner ...*"If you stay until everyone else is gone the last pair will be yours!"*

My friends were frantic:

- *"Poor you.... This is so unfair... You were so much looking forward to skiing today in this great environment!"*

I was undisturbed:

- *"Please go off and enjoy yourselves. I'll ride the chair down and get another pair! It is such a nice day and there is such a beautiful view! Go! ...Go and enjoy your skiing!"*.

I did enjoy myself. I met people that I would not have met otherwise. I rejoiced at the opportunity to do something unexpected...and my friends were very surprised indeed.

Rejoice on anything you can and elevate the mood of those around you. Consider it a mission in life to rejoice and help others do so as a consequence.

Take stock of all the positive energy available to you from so many sources and rejoice! It is a great Stress buster!

SHAKEN, NOT STIRRED!

When James Bond goes to the bar and asks for a Martini in his preferred way, it is "shaken, not stirred!".

I feel that this preference reflects the character of 007. Quite a few things happen to him and shake him but to stir him takes rather a lot.

Let us become followers of 007! Not to the bar, but turning this motto "shaken, not stirred!" into the way of life.

I have a tool to offer you: **the mental, invisible snowplough.**

A snowplough is designed to protect a vehicle, to open a way forward and disperse around it the obstacle represented by the snow so as to clear the road and allow us to move on.

Just imagine that you are on a snowy slope, on a sunny day. Suddenly, and quite unexpectedly something bad happens... you have an avalanche coming your way with terrifying power and noise.

Now imagine that you can instantly snap in place, between you and the avalanche, an invisible, powerful snowplough to deflect the flow of oncoming snow. You will end-up shaken, but safe.

In the future, when identifying a stress attack, just visualise it as a snow avalanche and snap your snowplough into place. The events will unfold and you will have to take your share of corrective action but you will come out of the crisis a lot better, shaken, not stirred, and in much better condition to take further corrective action.

Such a visualisation may take a little practice for some but is very effective in minimizing the effects of a stress attack. I have heard excellent reports from users of the invisible stress-busting snowplough.

THE ENERGY BUBBLE

To radiate or not radiate.
That is your choice!

Some people are so attractive that we want to be close to them. We want to touch the people we love....and we want to stay away from people we have negative feelings about. How come we all behave like this?

The answer came when I accidentally discovered the existence of personal energy fields.

When we bought a house in France and noticed that there was dry rot in the base of the walls, the architect suggested that we consult Mr Rey. So we did. He came with a portable magnetometer and went around the house measuring micro magnetic fields in various areas of the house.

Then he drew on the floor plan the "comfortable" areas of the house. Outside these comfortable areas were...not so comfortable areas, and some really uncomfortable areas. For example he pointed at two armchairs in front of the fireplace. We had purchased the armchairs together with the house. Mr Rey told us that the one on the right was in a very good spot but the one on the left was in a bad spot.

He also pointed out that there was a good spot about one meter to the left of the bad spot.

(Later I was able confirm with the previous owners that they both loved the armchair on the right but when compelled to use the left one they would invariably move it about one meter to the left!)

I then asked Mr Rey if his machine could read people's

energy fields as well. To my surprise he beamed a glorious smile and was happy that I asked. He proceeded to demonstrate that each person has his/her own field, which varies in intensity from person to person. Fascinating stuff!

But the most fascinating was that I later found that the intensity of the field will vary according to the people's emotions....and that it can be demonstrated visually with a divining or dowsing rods.

I immediately acquired good dowsing rods and have since been demonstrating the growth of the energy field when the person is thinking about something they love ...and its complete disappearance when the person is mentally focusing on a negative / sad idea.

This means that when we focus on the dark side of life and the unpleasant dimensions of any situation, our vital energy field disappears, which renders us immediately unappealing to anyone near us.

Conversely, if we focus on the positive side, on what can be done and will be done, we radiate energy and anyone close to us will feel it and react to it, albeit unconsciously.

To radiate or not to radiate ultimately depends on YOU!

ENJOY YOUR FOOD !

Do we enjoy all the food that we eat? Three times a day? Can you imagine a situation when half or three quarters of the food that we eat would not physically nourish us and would simply go through our body without contributing to its nourishment! Unthinkable isn't it?

Yet at an emotional level we take very little advantage of the precious moment when we put food in our mouth and could feel an array of textures and flavours.

We could be visualising all the good that this food brings to us.

We should be thankful for all the work that has gone into making it possible, the dozens of people who contributed to it.

When we do that, the food brings us much more than its calories, minerals fibres, vitamins, etc. It also brings joy and gratitude.

Gratitude, anyone?

In my home, we regularly offer a short prayer before every meal. Even on my own I do it. The benefit is to focus my mind on the joy to have such a meal, to be thankful for its presence, to prepare myself to get more out of it. The secondary benefit is that we also add a prayer for the people in pain or in crisis and we try and share some of our positive energy with those who need it.

Recently we were visited by our daughter and grand children. The eldest grandson was 5 years old. He discovered this ritual with great joy. It seemed that the ritual itself was already nourishing him. Since then, back in his home in the

Netherlands, he regularly asks his parents to say such a short prayer at the beginning of the meal. When the prayer is not said at the beginning he usually requests it when he realises it was not said.

Here is a child relying on his unpolluted feelings to identify what is good for him.

BELIEF PRECEDES EXPERIENCE

Thirty years in the advertising business have certainly taught me that what we are prepared to believe definitely shapes and colours our perceptions.

Blind tests of comparable products often do not show very clearly marked preference for one product vs. the other. Yet when the advertising concept is shown before the product is tested, the consumer's beliefs about the brand or its past history come into play as much as his reaction to the words and images.

Consider the care that is put into designing a packaging, in decorating a waiting room or lighting up candles and arranging flowers in a vase. These actions will shape the perceptions of those who will come in visual contact with these things. The words, colours and images on the pack will lead our thoughts in the required direction. The friendly and comfortable waiting room announces a caring organisation. The lit candles convey relaxation and love...and so do the flowers.

To a degree, this is what is involved in self-fulfilling prophecies.

Numerous authors have documented the fact that our mindset has an enormous influence over our perceptions.

- The way we look at children is totally different whether they are ours or someone else's. Every parent will have been pleased but a little surprised to hear friends singing the praise of one's children.
- A candle lit table will offer a nicer meal, whatever is in the plate. In our home, we light a candle for every

meal. Evening meal is traditionally special when candle lit but even breakfast has a tea-light beaming a signal of care and hospitality.

- A clean and orderly home is probably a better environment to live in. For that reason, investing some time in eliminating clutter and cleaning up any place is a stress busting activity.
- A clean car with a scent of freshness is probably a more tempting to buy than a dirty, messy, smelly one. It suggests that we shall enjoy our time in it.

What does this mean in terms of stress management?

It means that every time you are successful in thinking in terms of "*What can I do to improve on this situation? I know I can impact on this!*" you will empower yourself to act and you will do wonders.

So I invite you to lock up your inhibitions and fears and look at the bright side of things and **DARE**!

- Believe that whatever happens, you will learn.
- Whatever happens you will grow.
- Whatever happens you will win! It may not be the jackpot every time but you will gain experience, wisdom and confidence for the next round.

Looking on the bright side is the only way to undertake unpleasant things.

Think of the time when holidays end and it is "back to school" or "back to work" time.

So often, people will allow that inevitable moment to be filled with gloom and frustration.

Changing the perspective, changing the belief about what the moment could bring will make a tremendous difference.

KEEP THE BALANCE, SHED THE BALLAST

Remember the last time when you saw a tightrope artist. How could one be so balanced, so gracious, in the face of potential failure?

Would we ever be able to do such a thing?

Yes!

Indeed we are doing the same thing, or something very similar on a daily basis.

We are constantly paying attention in the selection of the next step, with a clear goal in sight, and having clear knowledge of the situation we are in.

In the physical training that I received in the French Chasseurs Alpins (Alpine Troops), one of the exercises was walking the full length of a long beam three meters above ground. Frightening exercise until one was able to accept and practice the advice to focus on the end of the beam and walk with confidence.

Those who succeed best at keeping their balance in life are those who are focused on the task at hand, without reducing their ability to perform by bringing unwanted ballast from one task into another.

They know how to commit to a task because they know when to disengage from that task.

Can you imagine a tight rope walker who would try to walk a length of cable while cleaning his glasses, while speaking on the phone to his or her partner and while worrying about the parking meter for his / her car?

He soon would be heading for disaster. He would have to simplify his life and put some order in his act.

Carrying ballast / baggage from one area of life to another is a poor habit that you must fight actively.

The White Tornado, later in the "Body" chapter, is a specific tool for this.

Balance your life.

Leave ballast behind and enjoy a life of less stress and more success.

READING ENERGY SOURCES

Are you aware of all the energy refuelling spots that are available around you?

Many computer games involve the idea of energy consumption and offer opportunities to replenish energy sources.

Anthony Willoughby, creator of the "I Will Not Complain" company, and a quite exceptional individual gives the following advice:

"Live with the 'Record' button on"

It is not as difficult as it may seem. And for the little effort that it requires, it delivers a huge return on investment.

In the coming days, try and read the energy of the people that you meet.

Read handshakes, read hugs, read body language, read beauty in people and environments, read the places where you are.

Let the energy, or lack of, reach you.

What are they telling you?

And please do not stop at receiving by reading. Become a larger energy source yourself! Try and transmit energy in the following way, suggested by Pai-Chang :

"Shut your mouth,
close your lips,
and say something!"

Such is the way to Less Stress and More Success!

Challenging and fun.

BE A HERO....
BUST A GHOST!

In my childhood, there was a wood that marked my memory. It was a somewhat dark place with tall trees that masked the sunlight by day and the moonlight by night.

To this day I wonder what there was in the forest and if it was so menacing and dangerous as to justify the fact that decades later I am still frustrated of not knowing.

In fact, I'll never know because bulldozers removed the wood and the frightening ghosts that laid there.

I recognised this memory when I heard the phrase:

"Where we focus our attention is where our beliefs will take shape."

Can we change the nature of our thoughts and therefore prepare ourselves to succeed where we would naturally doubt of our ability? I am convinced that we can.

The key to this is trust. In my coaching work, I regularly see clients achieving things that they thought to be out of their reach.

They say that my believing in their ability revealed that ability. Apparently, they suddenly were more able, because I gave them permission to achieve! Is this not truly extraordinary?

I am convinced that anyone can raise one's abilities by working on one's beliefs.

- If a negative or limiting belief is invading my thoughts, I must work on it. I must find the supporting evidence to that belief, before I can consider it as reasonably true. Because it could be nothing more than a received impression / opinion, and why should I be ruled by that?

- Whenever a limiting belief is at work in my mind, I have a fantastic opportunity to prove it wrong....IF I WANT TO.

If you have a ghost, a limiting belief of your own, be a hero, work on it and bust that ghost! I trust that you can.

It is not an easy task because it first requires that we accept that our belief is limiting. We may have lived with that belief for quite some time and admitting that we were ruled by such an erroneous idea may be difficult.

Then it requires that we muster the energy and the resolution to change it. To help us in such work we would be very wise to have a companion.

A professional Coach is the ideal companion to help you bust our ghosts.

THE WAITING GAME

Do you know of a very popular game.... in which every player is a loser?

Welcome to the Waiting Game.

Examine the following examples:

In the office:

Somebody sends around an invitation to a meeting and forgets to include you in the distribution list. When you realise that mistake you think:

- *"Again! Damn fool! He may not have done that on purpose but I do not care. I'll be missed at the meeting and ...they'll know that he made the mistake. The meeting can't come out well without me!"*

Count the losers in that example!

At home:

A sharp criticism, perhaps wrapped in a witty sentence had been dropped in the conversation and it hurts.

If you are on the receiving end of the blow, you may think:

- *"Fine!...you just wait!..."*

...and hold your tongue, throw peace to the dogs and brood.

If you are on the giving end of the blow and realise that you have just lost a major opportunity to be constructive, you may think:

- *"Damn! This was not very constructive!....but never mind! It will be for all the other times when I did not say anything. I am not the kind who asks for forgiveness"...*

... and also keep holding your tongue, hold your energy, throw your cool to the dogs and brood.

In both instances, you call Ego, Pride and Stubbornness to come and turn a small crisis into a big one...and furthermore, to bond this into a sticky situation you are prepared to give Ego, Pride and Stubbornness another ally: Time, the spice of the waiting game, the element that can turn ripples into tsunamis.

Don't wait! Heal it now!

Do it bravely, simply and gently. Like a true winner.

A French entrepreneur who worked with me was awestruck when he discovered that he had been practicing the waiting game – which he named "*la stratégie du pourrissement*" (the "rotting process strategy") – for so long, so systematically and with such poor results. He thought that the problem lied with the other people and letting things get worse would show them who was right!

No more waiting game for him!

He now operates with less stress and more success.

IT IS

YOUR

CHOICE!

PART TWO

HELPING YOUR BODY TO HELP YOU!

"I see my body as an instrument, rather than an ornament."

Alanis Morissette

" Can you identify your main tool in your line of work? "

I almost systematically ask this question to each of my clients.
I hear :
- *My computer*
- *My mobile phone,*
- *My organizer,*
- *My car, etc.*
I rarely hear the answer that you have already identified:
- "My body"

How unbelievably light-minded can we be? We rely on our body for everything, yet we take it for granted.

We know that it is vulnerable and a little fragile, yet we trust that it will resist, last, perform wonderfully and not wear-out too fast!

We heed the instructions manual for the car or the computer, but we ignore signals from the body, and as a result we accumulate tensions which produce toxins, which prevent us from functioning normally or even thinking straight.

How come?

Let's be serious, shall we?

This section is all about what you can do with your body to free it from the side effects of stress, feel better, function better and live better...perhaps even longer!

BEING AWARE

If you take anything for granted, you stop noticing that it is there until it calls for your attention through an emergency.

We often believe that if we do not think about something, that will mean less source of stress!

Do you agree that a body-related emergency is the last thing that you need?

So do cultivate a good awareness of your body.

Listen to your body, read the signs that it is sending to you:

- Tiredness
- Poor hair quality
- Poor skin tone
- Bad digestion
- Diminished sex drive
- Floppy posture, etc

What will you do with the information that you receive?

How far should you go in the pursuit of the ideal?

How much mediocrity is acceptable?

If you are serious about living with less stress and achieving more success, you have to take an extreme care of that most important tool of yours.

Recipe for progress:
Listen to the body's eloquent and strident messages.

- Create some Body Time.

30 minutes a day (excluding meal times) is a minimum. During that time serve your body as best as you can.

Option 1

- **Sit still and listen to your sensations.**

In a quiet area, or in a place where you can be still for some time (a bus ride or a train trip will do) turn your full attention to your body sensations.

Start with the outer sensations such a points of contact with clothes, air on the skin or the hair, warmth or cold, etc.

Once you are capable of quickly scanning your outer sensations, try focusing on sensations below the skin : muscles, tensions, heart beat... Listen to your body parts.

Take the body parts one at a time, in order and discover new knowledge about yourself.

Option 2

- **Take a close look at what you see in the mirror.**

We often do not look at our body in the mirror. Whether dressed or naked, few of us like to look at our body. Yet why hide from the truth? We can only deceive ourselves.

The objective is not to be ashamed of what we look like. To be ashamed is not very constructive. Looking in the mirror only serves a purpose if we decide to do something about what we see.

This regular critical look at ourself will identify potential areas for improvement.

The key is to be aware and to make conscious decisions to either accept the current state of things or make an action plan. Any action plan!

Option 3

- **Ask a good friend to give you a critical review.**

When our eldest daughter was 14, one morning in May, she saw me in my underwear and said:

- *"Daddy!, in 2 months we'll be on the same beach, you and I!"*
- *"Yes darling...and..?"*
- *"Well, I would prefer not to be ashamed of your waistline!"*

Why ask a friend?

Because you cannot be a good judge about yourself. One is often either complacent or too harsh on oneself. You need to hear the opinion of someone who likes you enough to be honest.

Will he / she be honest?

If you ask for honesty, you have a bigger chance to get it than if you do not. Make it a constructive request for support and assistance in your crusade to treat your body better. My daughter was kind enough to acknowledge that I had put the two months to good use...and I was very pleased with that feedback.

What will you learn that you do not already know when you ask someone else's opinion?

You will gain another point of view! It is always refreshing, although you can expect it to be challenging.

If you hear things that you already know, perhaps it says that you have grown complacent about the way you treat your body and it will be a good thing to realise that.

In any case:

- Write in a notebook the findings / problems to tackle.
- Decide on an objective for improving the condition.
- Identify "baby steps" that are easy to take so that you do not become discouraged.

• MUSCLES, MUSCLES !

We are animals.

Our body is designed to operate in animal conditions, with muscles working, requesting that the cardiovascular systems be fit and able to serve them, with a digestive system bringing the nutrients that our body needs.

Yet, we live less and less like the animals that we were created to be. The result is that the body that we were given is not used in the way that fits its needs.

Our skeleton needs muscles to keep it aligned and functioning well.

Muscles that are not used waste away, loosing their tonus, their strength and eventually becoming virtually useless.

When the muscles that are supposed to keep our body in check weaken, our posture changes. Soon, our backbone loses its optimal alignment. Pain is coming after.

- A bigger tummy pulls towards the front and creates extra pressures and tensions.
- A poor head position strains the neck and back muscles.

Muscles that are not used accumulate tensions and toxins.

The difference between a couch potato and a panther is obvious. What about the difference between someone fit and someone unfit? Less obvious outside, perhaps, but a huge difference in the way they feel and handle stressful situations.

Training for resistance and stamina need not be painful.

Just think of all the times when you could use your body instead of a powered “something”.

Afterthought.

How do you choose your food?

You are what you eat and drink.

There is food good for the body and food far less good for it.

You have to be the judge of what you feed to your body.
Just remember that when filling-up the tank of your car you do not use soft drinks, colas or cocktails or frying oil. You select the right pump with the right fuel.

Do you want your body's engine to run smoothly?

Some books about better food are listed in the bibliography, at the end of the book.

FRESHENING UP!

Refreshing our body regularly is a must.
Tensions build-up in the body, which restricts it's ability to function well.

Here are a few things that you can do to help protect your body:

Working with computers?

1- Rinse your hands in cold running water frequently. Every hour if you can. Place your hands up to the wrist under cold running water for a few seconds.
2- Look up and move your head up, down and around.
3- Blink frequently.
4- Move you eyes up and down and around.

Deskbound? Move!

Get up and shake a leg, move your shoulders and rotate your waist.

Better still, start a **shoulder massage** culture in your workplace.

I worked in Germany for 6 months and I noticed that my team was really tired in the afternoon so I started offering shoulder massages to those who wanted it. There was demand, and at about 60 seconds per person it was a great time investment.

They learnt how to do it to each other and the team spirit soared.

Leave the work-related trouble at work.
Take a White Tornado Shower on the way-out!

Imagine!

Get yourself one of these imaginary White Tornadoes. It comes in an invisible box that you mentally affix above the exit door frame of your workplace.

On the way out, you stop for a fraction of a second under the box on the door frame, mentally activate the tornado which drops down, spins around you and takes to the floor all the stress, the worries and the hassles of the day.

You are now free to go and enjoy the balance of the day, free to be a joyful friend or partner, free to take maximum advantage of your personal time.

Should you be afraid to lose the stress, worries and hassle, don't worry. They will be ready for you to pickup, if you so wish, the next day when you come in!

The White Tornado is guaranteed to work if you use it well and regularly. Any dissatisfied customer is entitled to full refund of the tornado's purchase price. No questions asked.

POSTURE

" Up and Forward! "

Does this sound like a slogan?
It is fairly close to the historical slogan of the Mexican PRI party "Arriba y Adelante"...but this is not a political debate.

In our context, *"Up and Forward!"* is the motto that I offer you to guide you through less stress, leading to more success.

The principle is inspired by the Alexander Technique and I encourage you to read one of the many books on the subject (There is a suggestion on my website, www.less-stress-more-success.com in the Books and Music section.)

"Up and Forward!" is about a way to use your head.
To use it physically that is! You should have it leading your spine upwards.
It aims at getting you to relax the neck muscles that tend to tighten-up when stress hits you.

Think about your neck muscles for a few seconds. Focus on them and feel them.
Is the back of your neck relaxed and the back of your head as far from your shoulders as it could be?

If not, you are keeping unwanted and unnecessary tension in your neck and shoulders, and you are not giving to your body a good chance to work well for you.

You may also not look as good as you would if you head was 'Up and Forward'

"Up and Forward!" is a rather precise motto. Please pay attention to the order of the movements. If you should opt for *"Forward and Up"* you would end up looking at the ceiling and having problems with your neck. Perhaps even a pain!

The right way is "*Up" first*. The head is lifted up as by an invisible string. You may want to consider that this string is held in the hand of God, or your Guardian Angel or whoever is gently watching over you to help you enjoy your life more.

That string is gently pulling you up to help you improve the way you feel and the way you look.

Your head should move freely sideways and forward/backward, gently. That freedom of movement is the indicator that the head id not pulled down by unwanted tensions.

Then comes "*Forward*".

When you raise your head, it will naturally tilt forward to keep your eyes level. That is good and will make you look very good. If you add a smile from the eyes...success is coming your way!

So, "*Up and Forward*" will lead you to be less stressed, and perhaps to more success too.

• WORK ON YOUR WRINKLES: SMILE WITH YOU EYES !

Here is a formidable tool to prevent tension build-up.

Work on your wrinkles! Since we are all going to have some wrinkles at some time, let's have good, positive ones which make our faces enjoyable to look at.

Smile! Every time you do, you are working on your future appearance.

And as a bonus, you are doing a lot of good to people around you.

There are many kinds of smiles.

The most effective and most relaxing is smiling with your eyes.

Look at some of the celebrities flashing their teeth to the camera. Look at the eyes and read the true intentions behind the smile.

Smiling with the eyes is the catalyst to a bigger, deeper, fuller smile.

Smiling with your eyes is challenging at the beginning, as you wonder how to do it. Some people are very sceptical about it and even doubt whether it is even possible to do it. Do try, and do persevere. I have no doubt that you will acquire it very quickly. You will get immense rewards from doing it and you will never want to stop!

Smile for Less Stress.
Smile for a beautiful face.
Smile for More Success!

BREATHING TACTICS

There are many ways to breathe and you can learn from many schools, whether it be yoga, meditation, martial arts etc. The following three techniques have specific purposes. If you learn them you will probably never use a sleeping pill again, you will rely less on coffee for an energy boost, and probably never lose your calm again.

1 – The basics:

The breathing cycle is like the washing machine cycle.

1 - In comes the clean air.
2 - While inside it does a cleaning job.
3 - Out goes the soiled breath, carrying away the unnecessary toxic material

And so on, forever, until the last cycle.

The comparison with the washing machine is useful because it calls us to identify the detergent that will clean our system during the breathing cycle.

In this case, it is in our mind, the desire to restore peace and quiet in our personal world.

Breathing without the awareness that it is a tool to manage our emotions is like a washing machine working with only water. Automatic but not terribly powerful.

One last but important thought: any good washing machine cycle starts with pumping out the potential deposit of water in the machine. It is the same in the breathing cycle. **It always starts on the exhalation!**

2 - Breathing for calm.

Any tension creates a blockage.

Most of the time, the first area where a blockage develops is the breathing.

Many people will hold their breath when concentrating on doing something difficult... but calligraphers often only write on the exhaling part of the breathing cycle. They have learnt that it is the best moment to use a stable hand.

Many people, when startled, will stop breathing, however briefly, and will have difficulties catching their breath afterwards in order to return to a normal state of mind.

By focusing on your breathing cycle in different circumstances, you will familiarize yourself with it and be better prepared to take control of it when required.

Train your breath to serve your purpose by learning to breathe consciously. Breathing slowly will restore calm in you.

When you are hit by an accidental rocking of your emotions, your breath will naturally shorten and its pace will increase. Try and counteract this increased activity. Exhale slowly through the mouth while visualising that you exhale the tension that you have just been inflicted. Then inhale slowly through the nose and exhale slowly again.

The result will be a more focused and calm state leading to better thinking, better reactions, less stress and more success.

An additional element for soothing the emotions is to

visualise that the air you inhale goes down, down beyond your diaphragm, very low into your abdomen.

3 - Breathing for sleep

This tip has come to be a blessing for many people who attended my "Less Stress, More Success" seminars.

It is about getting back to sleep at anytime but particularly at night.

I have met many people who challenged me and said *"This may not work for me. I never sleep well at night and sometimes sleeping pills don't even work!"*...Well none of them has come back to tell me that it did not work for them, and some of them e-mailed me with gratitude and surprise. *"It works! I sleep like a baby now!"*

The formula is quite simple: **X=[8+4+7) x2] x3**

You do not need a scientist's brain to figure it out. Let me explain:

Go back to the idea of the breathing cycle:

- Exhale slowly, though the mouth, on the count of 8. You can count fast or slowly, but you will have to maintain the same pace throughout the exercise, as the counting is to help you pace your breathing.
- This exhalation is the key to your relaxation and has to be complete. Moreover, as you exhale your mind will concentrate on the relaxation that it induces

- Inhale fully on the count of 4. Inhale through the nose.

- Hold your breath on the count of 7. This is the time when the "detergent" works on your tesnsions and your toxins.

That is the **(8+4+7)** part of the equation.

Now the "**x2**".

There are 2 basic ways to inhale air into your body.

- You can either expand the chest cavity, stretching your chest without lowering your diaphragm... That is the thoracic breathing!

- Or you can lower your diaphragm and push your abdomen out in front of you, without expanding your thorax. That is abdominal breathing.

If you are not familiar with these two types, I recommend that you try each one a few times to experience how it feels. A good idea during that practice is not to mix both breathing types and mentally focus on either the thorax or the abdomen.

"**x2**" means that you will do the full cycle once in each breathing type.

- As you are breathing **into the thorax**, feel how your chest and back muscles stretch to accommodate the lung expansion. As you hold the breath, visualise and feel how the air dissolves tensions and cleans the area. As you exhale blow away the "dirt" and experience with delight the sinking feeling, the liquefaction of your body into the mattress or the sofa.

- As you are breathing **into the abdomen**, focus on your lower body and visualise again the air working and cleaning, releasing tensions and massaging the organs. As you blow air out slowly, eject tensions, stress and welcome the comfortable feeling that invades you.

In summary, you will repeat the full 8-4-7 cycle twice, once in the thorax, and once in the abdomen. It is a great feeling!

"x3" simply means that you will repeat all of the above 3 times.

Almost everybody is asleep before the end of the third cycle.

$$X=[8+4+7)\ x2\}\ x3.$$

It is that simple!

Have a good rest!

4 - Breathing for energy

Sometimes we want a boost of energy because there is a task at hand that needs to be done.

Two simple techniques are available:

Breathing up

In the opposite way to the one described at the end of the "breathing for calm" section, you visualise that all the air that you intake goes up into your skull, into your brain, provoking an enhanced state of readiness.

Just a few cycles should pump you up!

"Doggie" Breathing

Here the cycle is shortened to the minimum and emphasis

is on shallow thoracic breathing, panting like an out of breath animal.

An important difference lies in the fact that you are not just panting to catch your breath with the intention to return to normal... but you intentionally sustain this breathing for up to 60 seconds, drawing and exhaling strongly and fast.

Should you experience dizziness, stop immediately as you may be hyperventilating and that could induce fainting.

5 – The straw that SAVES the camel's back

You probably heard the expression:

"That's the straw that broke the camel's back!"

It meant that some little, apparently insignificant thing, when added on top of the entire previous burden, made it unbearable and the whole thing collapsed.

Well! I have good news for you! This straw is the opposite one. It is a technique to make the whole load lighter to bear and easier to manage.

It goes like this: when some unexpected, unpleasant thing happens and you are startled, upset and feeling that this is a definite "stress attack", reach for that straw that will save your camel's back.

That straw is exactly like the straw that you would use to drink a cool drink on a hot summer day....except that it is not real.

When the stress attack hits, exhale! ...Exhale through the imaginary straw, so that only a small flow of air escapes from your mouth. Feel the air escaping slowly and know that you are regaining your composure.

Exhale fully trough the straw, until you have no more air in you. Then inhale normally, and if necessary exhale again through the straw. As you exhale, you have the time to think and prepare a better response than if you had rushed into a full blown immediate reaction.

That little imaginary straw will not only allow you to be better at reacting adequately to stress attacks. It will also be a signal to people who might be the origin of these stress attacks that you are not enjoying their contribution and are making conscious efforts not to antagonise them more than necessary. They will learn to read the sign and when you use the straw in front of them it will be a powerful signal to them.

GET RID OF THE TENSION

You may become very skilled at deflecting your stress attacks, but alas, every stress attack deposits some tension in you and you will always have to battle the accumulation of tension in your body.

We review here a few techniques to get rid of the tensions that accumulate.

1 - The White Tornado

The White Tornado is explained earlier in the chapter. It is based on the deliberate intention not to carry work tensions over into your private life, or vice versa.

2 – Stretching

Stretching is excellent to dissipate tensions, at any time of the day, but it is particularly important at the start and finish of the day.

In the morning, before getting out of bed give your whole body a decent wake-up stretch. Hands, wrists, arms, shoulders, back, neck, lower back, abdomen, thighs, calves, ankles and toes!

The "Full Monty" of stretches. All cats do it, even big cats like tigers and lions. It helps them to perform and be in shape. Do the same!.

In the evening, in bed, stretch again, gently and slowly. Feel the tension slipping away form your muscles. You will wake up so much more refreshed!

3 - Walking Lightly

This is a simple exercise which you can do inconspicuously and from which you will derive much well-being.

It works by helping you getting rid of that tension accumulated in the body. Most frequently tension accumulates in the neck / shoulders area, or in the lower back / gut area.

The exercise aims at getting you to identify when you have tension in those places and to get rid of it simply and effectively.

First, think about the sensation of having that tension in the body. If you focus on it you can identify that rigidity, that sensation of having a solid block where there should really be articulations working freely, operated by supple muscles.

Walking lightly is about deciding to get rid of that tension and doing it.

Get on your feet and find a space where you can take 20 to 30 steps in a straight line.

As you take the first steps, feel the tension in the shoulder / neck area, and decide that you will focus on it, and after three steps you will let that tension drop to your waist level and feel free in the shoulders and necks...and do it! One!...Two!... THREE!

As you take the next few steps feel how free your shoulders and neck are. Move and shake these shoulders and enjoy that new sensation of freedom!

If you have been successful at freeing your shoulders and neck, do not stop there. Take another three steps and decide to drop all the tension at waist level down to your heels and with every contact between heel and ground ...dissipate the tension into the ground.. Ready?... One!... two! ....and three!

Feel the tension leaving your body and dissipating into the ground.

Now you are walking lightly! Enjoy the feeling. Remember that most enjoyable moment.

It is however a feeling that has to be cultivated.

Tensions will silently return, and unless we are watchful, they'll settle again in their favourite places and we'll be diminished in our enjoyment of life.

So the message is twofold:

1 – Walk frequently

2 – Walk lightly every time you walk!

"Walking is man's best medicine".
Hippocrates (460 BC - 377 BC)

"It is no use walking anywhere to preach unless our walking is our preaching."
Saint Francis of Assisi (1181 - 1226)

4 – Dance with your Spine!

Flexibility is simply wonderful.

Watch anything flexible while it is moving. From bamboos in the wind, to pole dancers, flexibility is associated with vitality and life.

If stress takes you in its grip, it will tighten your muscles, reduce your flexibility, and that reduction will show mostly in your spine. You will not bend easily, and when you move, your torso will be fairly rigid.

You must try and prevent this from happening and an easy way is getting in the habit of dancing with your spine.

Be aware of your spine and move!

Move your hips, bend forwards and backwards, twist and stretch. Feel your spine as you do this and develop your own dance.

Put on some music, or just take advantage of music you can hear....or if necessary sing in your head and dance with your spine. Do it anywhere: at home, at work, in the bus, or the subway...just do it!

NOTE: Should you have any medical reason not to dance with your spine, consult with your doctor before you start doing the exercise.

GET RID OF THE TOXINS

Toxins are by-products of our activity. They are the waste that our body needs to get rid of in order to work well. They accumulate in our body until we take action to facilitate their elimination, mostly through urine.

As the blood travels through the body, it collects toxins and takes them to the kidneys for elimination. Then either the kidneys have the opportunity to discharge the toxins through urine, or they accumulate.

In the 1980's Vittel, a leading brand of mineral water in France, ran an advertising campaign which said that when the water flows slowly, the pipes and faucets get clogged. The visual in the ads was a line drawing of a man's face sadly looking down. Whether one read a concern for his plumbing or for his performance was up to the reader.... But the campaign did relaunch the water consumption habit in a country more prone to drinking wine than water. To this day, the effect is still ongoing.

I remember an advertising campaign in the Paris Metro subway trains in the late 50's which was recommending a moderate wine consumption in the amazing following way:

" Drink with moderation!
No more than 2 bottles per person per day!".

Today, the buzzword of people interested in promoting a healthier life is

8 glasses of water a day

Drink Water?

Does the idea of drinking water surprise you?

The more it surprises you, the harder you will probably have to work to get your body to help you to live with less stress.

Walking around, jogging or even working at your desk with a bottle of mineral water is not an awkward sight today. Asking for a glass of water instead of a coffee is not rare anymore.

If you do not drink water regularly, you may be a laggard rather than a leader. How do you feel about that idea?

Does the taste of tap water turn you off?

For those concerned about buying bottled water and having to carry it home, there are now very simple filter systems that deliver clean tasting drinking water on tap. We installed one in all the houses we have owned in the last ten years and it was always a good feature to show to potential buyers. Beyond the convenience of having clean tasting water on tap, it was the sign of a house where living well was high on the agenda of the owners.

Body Program Summary.

Your body is your most important asset and your main tool in working towards a life with less stress and more success.

Keep it in mind

- Listen to its messages.
- Monitor the way it works for you.
- Make special efforts to make it feel good!

Feed it well.

- Right foods, few stimulants, lots of water.
- Quality before quantity.

Give it rest and recreation.

- Proper sleep patterns.
- Keep it clean, both inside and outside.
- Lead it into meditation.
- Laugh daily. .

Give it the exercise that it needs

- Bust the tensions
- Create opportunities to change pace and move.

Give it the right tools to serve you:

- Comfortable clothes.
- Good environment.

Treat your body as the best friend that it longs to be.

PART THREE

WHAT IS AROUND YOU?

"When I grow up,
I will live in a lovely place,
full of light
and flowers,
beautiful things
and positive energy!"

You at age 10?

WARNING:

**You are about to enter a challenging topic and your comfort zone may be stretched.
Enter only if you are serious about living a better life!**

Otherwise skip this chapter and go to Relationships in the next section.

Please note that you will not get a rebate for turning away from realities and deciding to ignore this whole area of your life.

You decided to stay on course and take a serious look at how your environment can help you live better! Congratulations. I'll help you.

If any place does not support you, work for you and help you be at your best, whether for work or pleasure, I invite you to change it!

I am not saying that you should change places and move. I am saying: "do something about it so that it does work for you!"

Some places "feel" good and others do not. If you listen to your feelings, your sensations, you will intuitively know. We enjoy being where it feels good, where we do not expend energy fighting the environment. More of our resources are free to be focused on enjoyable and fulfilling activities.

Living with Less Stress requires that you identify and minimize the elements in your environment which do not support you. Similarly it requires that you maximize those elements that do support you. These actions will enhance the conditions for More Success.

I invite you to wake up to your environment, identify the good, the bad and the ugly around you and decide what you want to do and can do about it.

The process is simple, with 5 steps:

1. Becoming aware of your specific environment.
2. Deciding whether it fits your aspirations / requirements.
3. Determining action plans to improve your environment.
4. Taking action.
5. Enjoying your new environment will be the last and long lasting step.

Welcome to this powerful trip!

I invite you to have a fresh look at where you live and where you work / spend most of your time daily.

We'll take a cold look at anything that impacts on the quality of your life from the "outside". You will develop a fresh perspective on many physical aspects of what surrounds you.

With a pencil in hand, take the time to go slowly through the next few pages and to give as full answers as possible, writing them in the white space provided.

Environment evaluation:

Please answer honestly the following questions with a rating reflecting your candid opinion today. The rating will be between 1 (= totally negative) and 6 (= totally positive). There is no neutral point on the scale and you are invited not to attempt to be neutral /create a 3.5 rating.

The purpose of the exercise is to get you to confirm if you are positive or not about your environment.

Environment checklist.

Every time you look at a place to conduct the evaluation go through the following list before you cast a rating.:

- General atmosphere of the place
  (excluding the people who live there)

- Efficiency and friendliness of lighting

- Quality and quantity of air.

- Aesthetics / colours / decoration etc.

- Materials (flooring, fabrics, walls coverings etc.)

- Sound

- EMF/ Electro Magnetic Fields.

If you are unsure about the nature and location of electro Magnetic Fields, skip this criteria until you have a better knowledge about these and their causes.

YOUR HOME

- Are you happy with the dwelling where you live(1-6)?
  - Overall rating
- Is the place welcoming and supportive? (1-6)
  - Overall rating
- How does it impact on you when you come in? (1-6)
  - Overall rating
- What do you like most when you enter?

- What do you dislike most?

- Do you long to be there? (1-6)
  - Overall rating

- How "magical" do you feel your home to be? (1-6)
  - Overall rating

- List the words that describe the main components of you home's "magic".

Should you want to improve it, list, in order of importance for you, 3 things that you would do?

How determined are you to do something about it? (1-6)

List the obstacles that might prevent these changes from happening. Do list all of them even if they are small:

Place an asterisk(*) next to the obstacles that it is in YOUR power to remove.

Once you have done that, make an action plan to remove the obstacles... AND SHARE THAT PLAN with someone! If you have a Coach, this is ideal territory for Coaching sessions to help you plan and take the action.

Final recommendations about your home:

Love that place enough to invest in it
and make it work for you.

Wage war on Clutter

Clutter is your enemy.
Kill it before it strangles you.

- Clutter grows out of low commitment to the place where you are. ...and to yourself. You deserve better than clutter around you.

- Clutter hides the things that are useful to you.

- Clutter steals your time. It may look like it saves you time not to put things away but it is an illusion.

- Clutter accumulates dust and is bad for your health.

What defines clutter?

Anything which is not used frequently but is present near you is clutter. It can be papers on a desk, old magazines and newspapers, objects that have not been put away in their place, things stacked behind a door or under a desk, or on shelves.

All these things are probably the consequences of a tendency to leave things unfinished.

If you have clutter around you, try and trace it back to the unfinished business it emanates from.

The Chinese art of energy flow (Feng Shui) makes it a priority to eliminate clutter in order to promote a free flow of energy.

Do not tolerate inadequacies! Act now!

If you dislike anything in your home, try and fix it or move it out of your sight. It is important not to build tolerations about a place where you are supposed to refresh your energy and feel good.

Highlight beauty wherever you find it!

Identify the things that lift your spirits in your home and highlight them.

The traditional Japanese aesthetics favour a very bare environment, in a style that we have come to call Zen.

There is a double benefit to that: no clutter and when a painting, a sculpture, a souvenir, a flower arrangement or other special object is present, it is very visible.

So love your place
and treat it well!

Love it or leave it!

LOOK AT WHERE YOU WORK...
your daytime place.

Are you happy with the environment where you work?(1-6)

- Is the place welcoming and supportive? (1-6)
- Rate the place itself
- The systems that allow you to perform there
- The people:
- Management
- Colleagues
- Subordinates
- How does it impact on you when you first walk in? (1-6)
- What do you like most when you get there?
- What do you dislike most?

Do you long to be there? Is it attracting you? (1-6)

How magical is your workplace? (1-6)

- List the words that describe the main components of your workplace's magic.
    - .
    - .
    - .
    - .
    - .
    - .
- Should you want to improve it, what would you do to it, in order of importance for you?
    - .
    - .
    - .
    - .
    - .
- How determined are you to do something about it? (1-6)
- List the obstacles that might prevent these changes to happen:
    - .
    - .
    - .
    - .

Please place an asterisk(*) next to the obstacles that it is in your power to remove, even if your influence appears very small.

Once you have done that, make an action plan to remove the obstacles... AND SHARE THAT PLAN!

If you have a Personal Coach, this is ideal territory for Coaching sessions to help you plan and take the action.

Love that place enough to make it work for you!.

Out with the clutter and make room for highlighting elements that really work for you and help you work better.

If you do not love it...
and cannot leave it...

make sure that you do ALL you can
to eliminate your tolerations!

YOUR CLOTHING AND YOU

There are two main areas to consider when you think of how clothing impacts on your stress levels:

- The nature of the clothes you wear close to your skin.
- The freshness of these clothes
- The self-care that you express through the clothes you wear

The nature of the clothes you wear

I am not objective in this area.

I know that in terms of cost and convenience, man-made fabrics definitely deserve to be considered.

I accept that it is easier to care for a garment when it is man-made.

In fact I wear man-made fabrics on a regular basis, but in such a way that they do not touch my skin.

I am much more comfortable in natural fibre garments: Cotton is my favourite. Silk and wool are superb materials too....and softer wools are gentler to the skin.

My body breathes better in natural garments and whenever I have to wear man-made fabrics, I try to get back into cotton as soon as possible.

This is not to say that you should absolutely privilege such or such fabric. I thoroughly respect individual preferences. It is an invitation to listen to what your body tells you and pay attention to that message.

Freshness of the clothes.

If you can, I recommend that you put fresh, clean clothes each time you dress. It is a superb feeling. Try it! It is worth the effort.

- **A fresh pyjama each night is a great privilege.**

Whenever I cannot sleep with a fresh T-shirt every night, I turn the T-shirt inside-out for the second night. Besides encouraging the French custom that whenever you put a garment inside out you are about to receive a gift, it is also much more comfortable to the skin.

My family is very sceptical about the difference that it makes, but I feel the difference between the two sides of the fabric. I know that the perspiration of the first night has left a deposit on the inside of the T-shirt. I feel the difference when I slip it on for the second night.

- **A change of clothes at the end of the working day.**

What a great feeling when you can get to the end of your work time and freshen up for the balance of the day. I mentioned the White Tornado in earlier chapters. A physical shower, at the time of a change of pace together with a change of clothes is also a great luxury.

A shower before going to bed wearing clean, fresh nightwear, into a well made bed with fresh sheets and pillow cases is the ultimate luxury and the best way you can treat yourself to a super night's rest.

It may not be possible to reach such level of care for oneself on a regular basis but it is a very healthy objective.

- The self-care expressed by the proper management of your clothing says much about you. It is a way to support your body and your emotions. People notice it, even if subconsciously, and it sends messages about how much self-esteem you have.

When our son left home to go to College in Great Britain, we were living in Tokyo and I knew that I would have few opportunities to influence the way he was to live his life. I condensed my recommendations to him into two words that were to apply to all aspect of his life:

"BE CRISP!"

It was to apply to his clothing and to many other areas of his life away from the supporting family circle. It was to help him feel supported.

If your self-care speaks about you, it also speaks to you... Do listen to it and take time to see how you can get your clothing to work for you.

Some people are obsessed with impeccable and fresh clothes. Others are oblivious to stains and do not stop a second to think about how frumpy they look. The former may be stressed from their search for ideal perfection. The latter are probably not giving their body... and their life the best support it could get from their clothing.

The right attitude is somewhere in the middle and everyone will chose where for himself, whether consciously or not.

PART FOUR

To:

Jacqueline,
Maurice,
Marie,
Sophie,
Johanna,
Nicolas,
Léo,
Eliott,
Cedric,
Patrice,
Jerôme,
Rachel,
Alphonse,
José Luis,
Carmen,
Toshinao,
Susana,
Cristina,
Fernando,
Sumiko,
Luigi,
Ami,
Olivier,

Madeleine,
John,
Akim,
Isabelle,
Mary-Alice,
Louis-Eric,
Clive,
Anne,
James,
Lupita,
Zita,
Ladji,
My Guardian Angel,

Et les autres!

With my gratitude for their contribution to
my wisdom in managing relationships.

**“You cannot
lift a pebble
with only one finger”**

(Hopi proverb)

Do we need the other people?

Parents?
Teachers?
Grand-parents?
Neighbours?
Brothers and sisters?
Colleagues?
Bosses?
Subordinates?
Life Partners?
Suppliers?
Clients?

God?

What a bizarre question?
Do we have a choice?

But what if we need them
and it happens to be difficult to relate to them?...
How stressful!
Is there a way out of this stress?

YES!

We need these relationships...

...and
we need them to be
as rich
and as supportive
as possible.

If you claim that you do not need rich relationships and that you can live without the support of friends and relatives, here are a few questions for you:

- Has it always been like that for you?
- We all start with someone caring for us.
- If I tell you that it is ALWAYS possible to have a rich relationship with others, will you shut your eyes and stop reading?
- If you could rewind your life to the time when it started to be difficult to relate to others, would you change anything in the way you related to others?

This chapter offers simple ideas that can be very powerful instruments to fertilise your relationships with anyone and everyone.

Sometimes it looks like the others
have not understood that
it is a great joy
to have rich relationships.

Don't trust the appearances.
They may just be clumsy about handling relationships.

Truth #1:

It falls on us
to establish, improve, maintain
and enjoy
every relationship.

Would you like to hear more about a popular game which is played the world over and few people know about?

Do you remember the Waiting Game?

It goes like this:

One person upsets another. It does not have to be intentional. It just happens. The person who is upset usually calls on his/her ego to help formulate a strong and decisive response.

If you just had an argument, you focus on your own perspective. If your feelings are hurt you may react aggressively, or defensively, creating a conflict. A tension sets between you and the other party ....and you decide to wait for the other party to take the first step towards the resolution of the conflict....

If both parties are similarly trained, the Waiting Game will last a very long time... hours....days....weeks...months... years or lifetimes.

In my Coaching work, I have worked with clients who admitted unresolved disputes and tensions lasting over 10 years. 10 years of suffering. 10 years which could probably have been much better, without the effects of that wasteful Waiting Game.

The ugliness of the Waiting Game is that it has no winner, just losers. Nevertheless it is still played by millions.

The Waiting game is cultivated passivity.

Taking steps to resolve a dispute or a misunderstanding is a powerful act of generosity towards yourself as well as towards the other party

In the Benedictine monastic order, the rule of St Benedict dictates that one should not let the sun set on an unresolved dispute.

Truth #2

God has no other hands than yours for gestures that heal the people you come in contact with.

God has no other voice than yours to tell people how great they are.

God has no other eyes than yours to see where tolerance, mercy, gentleness and love will change the world for good.

Teaming up with God to make people happier is a source of immense joy.

So how can we, shall we play another relationship game?

Whilst the Waiting Game cultivates passivity, the new game is based on a proactive state of mind. With such an attitude you will find yourself caring more about what happens, about attracting good things and nice, positive people in your life and you will start consciously managing your relationships.

You will start with people close to you and important to you, but quickly it will expand to people that you see less often, or know less well. Ultimately, you will find yourself surrounded by almost exclusively pleasant people

Relationships are a living thing, like a flower, or a pet. If you take proper care of them they grow and flourish. If you neglect them, you soon notice the effect and suffer from it.

2 - Relationship buzzwords:

Pick two of the phrases below and see how often you can use them in the next 24 hours

- *Thank You!*
- *Mmm! This is good!*
- *I like the way you dress!*
- *That was great meal!*
- *I like to be with you!*
- *I like to work here!*
- *Your room looks so nice!*
- *Thanks for your help.*
- *Good job!*
- *You are the best... I know!*
- *I am so glad to have you on my team!*
- *I would be so happy if you would/could...*

3 - ATTRACTING GREAT RELATIONSHIPS:

Relationships are indeed a living thing.

People will want to have a relationship with you if you are attractive.

Laura Bergman Fortgang, a successful coach that I respect very much told me that there are three types of people, classified according on their effect on other people:

- **Rockets**
- **Floaters**
- **Sinkers**

Which type are you?

<u>Are you a "Sinker"?</u>

- Your company is a burden to other people.
- Your comments are probably negative or pessimistic most of the time.
- You are morally not attractive.
- It would be in other people's best self-interest to contribute to changing you...or to leave you alone. How is that for attractiveness?
- You should upgrade yourself to "Floater" or "Rocket" as soon as possible!

<u>"Floaters"</u> are not impacting others in any way. They do not have a positive effect on you but at least they do not have a negative one either. More often they have no interaction with you, or if they do it is in a neutral, harmless way.

<u>"Rockets"</u> are a powerful source of energy for you.

Perhaps it is through the ideas they have, or through their

energy levels, or because they care for you, acknowledge your good sides and make you feel good that they bring you energy.

They are a joy to have around. They are attractive!

Be a Rocket! ... You can.

Even if you are not considered a rocket by your friends and family, you can become one and increase your attractiveness.

You will have to want to be one, though. In order to help you grow into a Rocket, use the following tips:

1. **Acknowledge** the good side and good actions of everyone you meet.

Most psychologists agree today that the impact of acknowledgement on people's emotions is big. It helps them feel respected, liked and often even loved.

2. **Smile with your eyes**.

The first contact that you have with people is through the eyes, so this is where you have to learn to smile.

When your eyes smile, the whole of you is smiling too, from the face to the posture and soon the friendly empathetic words follow.

Smiling with your eyes is not easy but well worth practicing. You can smile with your eyes before smiling with the rest of the face. It flows naturally from an attitude that you develop towards people.

Once you will are skilled at smiling with your eyes, try smiling with your voice!

3. **Listen** intensely.

When a couple stops talking to each other, it is a big drama, yet few are conscious of the moment when they stop listening to each other.

Listening is a critical element in any relationship. Whenever we do not listen intensely, completely, with a genuine desire to understand what the other person is trying to communicate we are already living a relationship at a level below its full potential.

When training professional Coachs at the Instituto Internacional OlaCoach (Madrid, Barcelona or Bogotá) I lead aspiring Coaches through intense drills on the three identified levels of listening....and these students admit that being listened to at the deepest level is a very rich moment never experienced before.

They also bear witness to the impact on their own lives of making efforts to listen better to their friends, colleagues, relatives and everyone in general.

When we let our own thoughts get in the way of understanding what someone else is trying to tell us, we muddy their message and we deprive ourselves of an opportunity to understand so much more.

What are the tips for listening at the richest level?

- **Silence**. When we are committed to silence, we make room; we create a space to hear, to perceive more.

- Don't worry about losing opportunities to express your point of view. Your turn to speak will come and the quality listening that you will have offered will have gained you extra credibility in the other person's mind. How much credit do we give to someone who interrupts us in the middle of a sentence?

- **Refraining from judging** the words, the ideas, the intention or the delivery. If we try to form an opinion early in the communication process, we instantly lose that special listening quality that we seek.

- Don't worry about not remembering enough to be able to respond. Your high attention to what is being expressed will give you plenty of material to form an opinion. The important is that this opinion will now be far more "educated" than if you had jumped to a conclusion early. Being better informed, your response will be much more receivable.

- **Opening up** to the person and the emotions that drive that person into saying what you hear. Be willing to hear anything. Be eager to understand where the person comes from. It is essential to be able to take into consideration what the person really wants to communicate.

- When we leave aside - or shut off – the emotional side of the communication, we risk misreading the message, but even worse we risk alienating the other person. How afraid can we be of hearing the facts - as perceived by the person we are communicating with? Why would we want to apply a filter to what they want to tell us? Opening up to perceiving all the components of a message does not imply that we shall have to accept that message as solid truth. We can still disagree with the ideas expressed....but if we are to disagree, let it be on the basis of a clear understanding of what the message is communicating.

- **Extending one's antennae** in order to perceive signals that otherwise will be lost: The breathing pace, the intonations, the eye movements, the body language, and importantly your own intuition are precious sources of valuable information.

4 - Manage relationships consciously

Relationships are living things. Ignored or left to their natural course, they are vulnerable and will lose strength and wither.

In the next pages are a few more ideas that will help you stay aware that the richness of your relationships ultimately depends on you:

- The Emotional Bank Account
- Giving
- Using go-betweens
- Nemawashi
- Valentine Everyday

a. The Emotional Bank Account

This is simple to understand for anyone who ever received a bank statement with an overdraft warning. The few others will have to imagine.

When we first meet someone and develop a personal relationship with that person, we open an emotional bank account. Each personal attention, gesture, word constitutes a deposit into the emotional bank account. While that account has a large positive balance, it produces an exceptional feeling of security and comfort.

In early stages of a relationship with someone we tend to make frequent and ample deposits. We are also able to make frequent and ample withdrawals on the account.

Unfortunately, security can lead to take things for granted and over time the frequency and size of the deposits will change. People who take a relationship for granted and stop making deposits might one day find an envelope with a sobering message. The account is in the red, or perhaps worse it is being closed.

Think about your two or three most important relationships, either personal or professional. What is the status of these accounts?

b. Give to everyone, everytime.

Doesn't this sound like a weird idea?
How could I give to everyone? ...let alone every time?

The idea is somewhat related to the "Waiting Game" that I mentioned earlier. If you want to be surrounded by happy people, you should work on it all the time because it will not happen by itself.

In my "Less Stress, More Success" live seminars on this theme I lead participants to understand the concept of a relationship currency. There is such a thing, and in order to receive, one has to create a flow, and hence to give.

From now on, whenever you meet someone, give them something. The simplest and easiest gift is a kind thought or a well-being wish.

If you are in a queue waiting for the cashier to process the purchase of people ahead of you, instead of focusing on the slow speed or the limited abilities of the operator, try sending a mental message to that person.

- *"You seem to have a busy day. Thank you for doing your best!"*
Make it personal if you can read her name badge:
- *"Hello Jane. I like your smile!"*
- *"Thank you for being there!"*

Any positive thought or message will do the trick. When your turn comes you will get a glorious smile...or some other sort of acknowledgement that you are more welcome than those before you. Try for yourself!

You can give a compliment, a card, a smile, a hug, special thanks, flowers, a raise, promotions and other more visible gifts, but do train hard to send dozens or hundreds of mental smiles and positive wishes every day. You will enjoy the difference that it will make in your own life.

c. The Go-Between

During my 12 years of work in Japan, I learnt a lot about relationships, and one of the major lessons was about the value of using a go-between when the direct communication is likely to be difficult.

The role of the go-between is so institutionalised in Japan that business introductions are often through a go-between who connects two potential partners. The very special dimension of that role though, is that the go-between is responsible for the quality of the relationship and is expected to be available to help defuse potential tensions between the two new partners.

The go-between has the opportunity to help both parties to think carefully about their position, and also is in a better position to express the other party's point of view without it sounding like a threat.

The personal Coach is a "half" go-between. Many of my clients discuss with me their challenges and difficulties, and in so doing allow themselves to examine the issues in a calmer environment. Spouses find a better way to put their views across, managers get an opportunity to think carefully about how they will present a case to their boss or run a meeting.

If you attend one of my "Less Stress, More Success" seminars, you will learn about Manuel and Franquette, our heroic V.G-B.'s who help us maintain harmony at home.

d. Nemawashi

In order for a relationship to proceed smoothly, the ideal is to have an operating consensus. Many people are afraid of the very idea of consensus because they fear that their individual position might be compromised or overruled by the diversity of opinions expressed during the search for a consensus.

Seeking a consensus, at its worst can lead to immobility; however there is no better thing than consensus when there is a leader.

The process to get to the consensus requires that everybody's perspectives and sensitivities be taken into consideration, that some negotiations take place and that in the end, all parties involved in the consensus agree to the selected solution. That process, in an open debate, can be very painful and very tiring. It sometimes leads to stalemates, with some of the parties reacting very negatively and influencing third parties.

A Japanese gardening practice has been adopted by Japanese businessmen to help reaching consensus in decision making. It is the "NEMAWASHI" (Neh-mah-wah-she).

In garden landscaping this practice is used to transplant a mature tree while minimizing the negative impact on the tree. One can see the parallel with imposing a change of practices or environment in a business.

In gardening as in business, the optimum situation is when the change is well accepted. Any effort to make the change more successful is justified.

For a tree, the technique involves cutting the root system around the tree one year before it is moved thus allowing the tree to get used to and adjust to a smaller root system before changing the rest of its environment. When the time comes to move the tree, it is easy to lift the tree with its new limited root system and transplant it successfully.

In business, it implies anticipating the potential debate that could arise in a meeting and discussing with all key parties individually before calling the general meeting with all parties involved.

The separate preliminary negotiations will have allowed taking divergent points of view into consideration.

An agreement will be reached faster, with fewer tensions, and lead to the majority, if not all of the parties leaving the meeting with a smile on their face.

The typical win-win situation.

One has to remember, however, that a consensus is reached around the ideas of the strongest party in the discussion, so if you wish to operate in the smooth environment of a consensus, it falls on you to prepare the ground with a proper and timely Nemawashi.

e. Valentine whenever!

If love is the ultimate relationship, the example of St Valentine is fascinating. My dictionary does not say why he is the saint patron of lovers, but it says that on Valentine Day we are supposed to offer a gift to the one(s) that we love or cherish.

Why is that thought valid?

Why on that day more than on any other?

Why is it limited to a day?

Can I not have a Valentine week or Valentine month to further improve my relationship with those which are important to me?

Let us lead intense and wonderful Valentine lives!

Afterthoughts.

Now that you have finished reading this book, are any of the ideas and tips that it contains going to stay with you?

As I run the "Less Stress, More Success" seminars to various audiences, I try and ask them 6 months later if any of the techniques that I have offered them is still serving them and how much their life has improved.

I find that among those who attend the seminar, rare are those who are not using one or another of the techniques.

I also find that those who used the summary of concepts that I leave behind as a reminder at the end of the seminar declare that their life has noticeably improved. They had taken better advantage of opportunities.

Changing habits that one developed over years or decades cannot be done overnight. It takes some persistence.

Some people believe they have inherited some traits of character and that they have to live with these even though these traits work against them. Experience proves that with real determination and work it is possible to change our ways.

Combining these observations led me to train as a Personal Coach. I came to Coaching because it appeared that with all the wisdom that I could offer in a 4-hour or a 7 hours seminar, it was only offering a one-time limited stimulus to the people that I was trying to help.

Through Coaching, I work with clients who are determined to live their lives at a higher level.

I can see through the weekly telephone conversations that those who stay focused on their evolution, those who use the tools that we discuss and design together for them fare far better than those who just brushed once against the opportunity to understand all we can do to help ourselves live a better life.

I wish that you will keep this light book as a companion. I dare to hope that you will share some of the tips, or recommend the book, to friends, colleagues and relatives and in so doing plant the seeds of a happier environment for your own life.

There are more tips and ways to live with less stress. They may be the subject of future books.

Should you have one that works particularly well or if you have any feedback on this book, do not hesitate to contact me at coach@less-stress-more-success.com

And of course if you are tempted by a boost to your life and want to be coached to get there faster and more easily than on your own, wherever you live, I shall be delighted to offer you telephone coaching from wherever I shall be enjoying my life at the time.

Fare well and thank you for your company.

Haitzpean – October 2006

Bibliography.

BEING

- **Eternal Echoes** – Exploring our hunger to belong
John O'Donohue – Bantam Books – ISBN 0-553-81241-6

- **Travelling Light**
Daniel O'Leary

- **The Prophet**
Kahlil Gibran – Pan Books – ISBN 0-330-26220-3

- **Living, Loving & Learning**
Leo Buscaglia,Ph.D. – Fawcett Columbine – ISBN 0-449-90024-X

- **Prescriptions for Living**
Bernie Siegel – Rider - ISBN 0-7126-7021-1

- **FLOW – The Psychology of Ultimate Experience**
Mihaly Csiksentmihalyi – Harper Perennial – ISBN 0-06-092043-2

FENG SHUI

- **Feng Shui, The Chinese Art of Placement**
Sarah Rossbach – Penguin Arkana – ISBN 0-14-019353-7

YOGA / BODY CARE / TAI CHI

- **EcoYoga,** practice and meditations for walking in beauty on the Earth

Sarah Rossbach – Penguin Arkana – ISBN 0-14-019353-7

TIME MANAGEMENT

- **Get Everything Done and Still Have Time to Play**

Mark Foster – Hodder & Stoughton – ISBN 0-340-74620-
3

FOOD

- **SUPER foods**

DK London – ISBN 0-86318-494-4
Michael Van Stratten and Barbara Briggs
The cookery book that combines recipes using delicious natural ingredients with a guide to the therapeutic properties of common foods to improve your health

- **Foods That Harm And Foods That Heal.**

Reader' Digest- ISBN 0-276 421930
An A-Z guide to safe and healthy eating

- **The Detox Diet Cookbook**

Lorenz Books – ISBN 0-7548-0473-9
Over 50 delicious recipes for cleansing the system and revitalising the body.

About the Author

Christian Worth is a citizen of the World. He grew in the Haute Couture environment, and was led at an early stage to cast an observing eye on the tribulations of being a well adapted human with a balanced life.

Until age 16 he suffered from a squint in the right eye which made eye contact difficult and left him with a nagging concern for whether his messages were being received.

For 3 decades he worked in the high pressure world of Advertising, taking his family away from France, successively to live in Mexico, Milan, Montreal, Tokyo, Frankfurt, Tokyo again, Hong-Kong and the United Kingdom.

He now lives in the Pays Basque, in the South West tip of France. He works on the telephone and Internet as a very successful Personal Coach with people who enjoy the eye that he casts on their challenges, the solid support that he offers and the stimulating questions that he asks.

He also teaches the fine art of Coaching at the Instituto Internacional Olacoach, in Madrid, Barcelona and Bogotá.

He offers his 4 hours seminar "Less Stress, More Success" to audiences around the world, in either in Spanish, English or French. The seminar has already toured London, Los Angeles, Montreal, Frankfurt, Madrid and Barcelona.

He is the author of three books in Spanish:

Abre el Melón
(with Jose Luis Menéndez)

Para Mi Esto!
(with Pilar Fariña Rodríguez)

Menos Estrés, Mas Éxito!

He can be reached at
coach@less-stress-more-success.com
www.less-stress-more-success.com

Made in the USA